# How Many A...

**Adria Klein**
**Illustrated by Loretta Lustig**

The little kittens had six mittens.

They lost some mittens.
How many are missing?

The little kittens had six socks.

They lost some socks.
How many are missing?

The little kittens had six boots.

They lost some boots.
How many are missing?

Did Mother find all
of the missing things?